SEQUENCES
ORDER MATTERS!

Lyrics by NADIA HIGGINS
Illustrations by SR. SÁNCHEZ
Music by DREW TEMPERANTE

CANTATA
LEARNING

WWW.CANTATALEARNING.COM

CANTATA LEARNING

Published by Cantata Learning
1710 Roe Crest Drive
North Mankato, MN 56003
www.cantatalearning.com

Library of Congress Cataloging-in-Publication Data
Names: Higgins, Nadia, author. | Sánchez, Sr., 1973– illustrator. |
   Temperante, Drew, composer.
Title: Sequences : order matters! / by Nadia Higgins ; illustrated by Sr.
   Sánchez ; music by Drew Temperante.
Description: North Mankato, MN : Cantata Learning, [2018]
Identifiers: LCCN 2017017514 (print) | LCCN 2017047225 (ebook) | ISBN
   9781684101719 (ebook) | ISBN 9781684101191 (hardcover : alk. paper)
Subjects: LCSH: Workflow--Juvenile literature. | Sequential
   analysis--Juvenile literature.
Classification: LCC HD62.17 (ebook) | LCC HD62.17 .H54 2018 (print) | DDC
   658.5/3--dc23
LC record available at https://lccn.loc.gov/2017017514

Book design and art direction, Tim Palin Creative
Editorial direction, Kellie M. Hultgren
Music direction, Elizabeth Draper
Music arranged and produced by Drew Temperante

Printed in the United States of America in North Mankato, Minnesota.
122017   0378CGS18

ACCESS THE MUSIC!

SCAN CODE WITH MOBILE APP

CANTATALEARNING.COM

TIPS TO SUPPORT LITERACY AT HOME

WHY READING AND SINGING WITH YOUR CHILD IS SO IMPORTANT

Daily reading with your child leads to increased academic achievement. Music and songs, specifically rhyming songs, are a fun and easy way to build early literacy and language development. Music skills correlate significantly with both phonological awareness and reading development. Singing helps build vocabulary and speech development. And reading and appreciating music together is a wonderful way to strengthen your relationship.

READ AND SING EVERY DAY!

TIPS FOR USING CANTATA LEARNING BOOKS AND SONGS DURING YOUR DAILY STORY TIME

1. As you sing and read, point out the different words on the page that rhyme. Suggest other words that rhyme.

2. Memorize simple rhymes such as Itsy Bitsy Spider and sing them together. This encourages comprehension skills and early literacy skills.

3. Use the questions in the back of each book to guide your singing and storytelling.

4. Read the included sheet music with your child while you listen to the song. How do the music notes correlate to the words of the song?

5. Sing along on the go and at home. Access music by scanning the QR code on each Cantata book, or by using the included CD. You can also stream or download the music for free to your computer, smartphone, or mobile device.

Devoting time to daily reading shows that you are available for your child. Together, you are building language, literacy, and listening skills.

Have fun reading and singing!

A **sequence** is a string of steps. The steps always go in order. One step happens first, and then comes another. What happens if you mix them up?

Turn the page and find out. Sing along to this silly song about sequences!

A sequence tells you what to do.
First step one and then step two.

Steps go in order. Keep them straight,
or things might not turn out so great.

Put on your socks. Next come your shoes.
Switch it around, you say?

Put on your shoes and *then* your socks?
You'll have the weirdest day!

A sequence tells you what to do.
First step one and then step two.

Steps go in order. Keep them straight, or things might not turn out so great.

Here comes the pitch. Now swing the bat.
Don't mix up how it's done.

First swing the bat, then throw the pitch?
This game is so not fun!

A sequence tells you what to do.
First step one and then step two.

Steps go in order. Keep them straight,
or things might not turn out so great.

14

Crack an eggshell. Plop it in.
Don't change the recipe.

Drop the egg, *then* crack the shell?
This meal looks too crunchy!

Use the toilet. Then
please flush.
Don't pull a **switcheroo**.

Flush the toilet and
then sit down?
Um, thanks, but
no thank you!

19

A sequence tells you what to do.
First step one and then step two.

Steps go in order.
  Keep them straight,
or things might not
  turn out so great.

Steps go in order.
  Keep them straight,
or things might not
  turn out so great.

21

SONG LYRICS
Sequences: Order Matters!

A sequence tells you what to do.
First step one and then step two.
Steps go in order. Keep them straight,
or things might not turn out so great.

Put on your socks. Next come your shoes.
Switch it around, you say?
Put on your shoes and then your socks?
You'll have the weirdest day!

A sequence tells you what to do.
First step one and then step two.
Steps go in order. Keep them straight,
or things might not turn out so great.

Here comes the pitch. Now swing the bat.
Don't mix up how it's done.
First swing the bat, then throw the pitch?
This game is so not fun!

A sequence tells you what to do.
First step one and then step two.
Steps go in order. Keep them straight,
or things might not turn out so great.

Crack an eggshell. Plop it in.
Don't change the recipe.
Drop the egg, *then* crack the shell?
This meal looks too crunchy!

Use the toilet. Then please flush.
Don't pull a switcheroo.
Flush the toilet and then sit down?
Um, thanks, but no thank you!

A sequence tells you what to do.
First step one and then step two.
Steps go in order. Keep them straight,
or things might not turn out so great.

Steps go in order. Keep them straight,
or things might not turn out so great.

Sequences: Order Matters!

Pop/Hip Hop
Drew Temperante

Chorus

A se-quence tells you what to do. First step one and then step two. Steps go in or-

-der. Keep them straight, or things might not turn out so great.

Verse

1. Put on your socks. Next come your shoes. Switch it a-round, you say? Put on your shoes and then your socks? You'll

have the weird-est day!

Chorus

Verse 2
Here comes the pitch. Now swing the bat.
Don't mix up how it's done.
First swing the bat, then throw the pitch?
This game is so not fun!

Chorus

Verse 3
Crack an eggshell. Plop it in.
Don't change the recipe.
Drop the egg, then crack the shell?
This meal looks too crunchy!

Verse 4
Use the toilet. Then please flush.
Don't pull a switcheroo.
Flush the toilet and then sit down?
Um, thanks, but no thank you!

Last Chorus

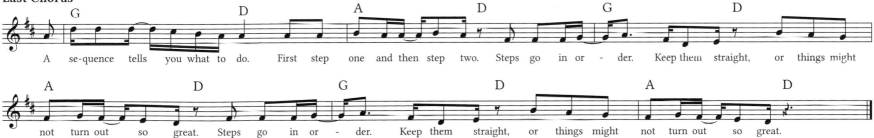

A se-quence tells you what to do. First step one and then step two. Steps go in or - der. Keep them straight, or things might

not turn out so great. Steps go in or - der. Keep them straight, or things might not turn out so great.

GLOSSARY

sequence—a series of steps that must happen in order

switcheroo—a funny mix-up

GUIDED READING ACTIVITIES

1. Make a timeline of your day. For example, write when you wake up, brush your teeth, and have lunch. Cut up your list, with one entry for each piece of paper. Mix up the pieces. Put them back into a sequence.

2. This song imagines mixing up everyday sequences. What are some other sequences you do? What would happen if you mixed up the steps?

3. Listen to the song again. Make up a dance routine to go with it. Draw pictures of your dance moves. Make sure they are in order!

TO LEARN MORE

Byous, Shawn. *Because I Stubbed My Toe*. North Mankato, MN: Capstone Young Readers, 2014.

Driscoll, Laura. *Count Off, Squeak Scouts!* New York: Kane Press, 2013.

Hoena, Blake. *Algorithms: Solve a Problem!* North Mankato, MN: Cantata Learning, 2018.

Hubbard, Ben. *How Coding Works*. North Mankato, MN: Heinemann-Raintree, 2017.

Lyons, Heather. *Coding, Bugs, and Fixes*. Minneapolis, MN: Lerner, 2017.